The Color of Water

Words of Praise

Powerful emotional journeys in this book—racial violence, the tragedy of war, forced human migration. The poem "Cape Fear" pierces the soul. McCormick places you in a slave auction at the Market House and summarizes it through the voice of Native Americans who connect the horror of the auction to their own imminent fate. — *Kimberly Smith, Assistant Professor of English and Digital Media, Elizabeth City State University*

McCormick invites you to a place of deep reflection. You weep when you read "Sweet Tea." What you hear will change your world view. Emotions rise in "Black Water" as you realize the water that gives us life can also be used as a weapon to oppress and take life away simply because of color. — *Sackeena Gordon-Jones, PhD, Author, Adjunct Professor North Carolina State University*

Rediscover the power of poetry in this authentic, thought provoking book! From the searing poem "Paperboy - Departure to Vietnam" to the racially provocative "French-African Ice Skater," this work is beautiful and courageous. Highly recommend for anyone who wants a deeper understanding of the human condition. Loved "Three Sister's Swamp and the Black River"! — *Christopher Hitch, PhD, Author, Professor St. Andrews University*

To understand and connect with social injustice around the world read this book! McCormick's poetry demonstrates what it means to really observe suffering to have empathy for "others." The use of imagery to understand people is extraordinary—read "Blue Heron" and "Woman of Rwanda." — *George Koonce, PhD, Marion University, Author, Life After Football, Super Bowl Champion*

Other books by
Horace McCormick Jr.

The Devil's Courthouse

Coming Winter 2021

The Color of Water

Poetry to Provoke Life and Heart

Horace McCormick Jr.

• WRITE WAY •
PUBLISHING COMPANY
RALEIGH, NORTH CAROLINA

The Color of Water
Copyright © 2020 Horace McCormick Jr.

Printed in the United States of America
ISBN 978-1-946425-57-7

Book Design by CSinclaire Write-Design
Cover Design by Klevur

• WRITE WAY •
PUBLISHING COMPANY
RALEIGH, NORTH CAROLINA

For Mary P. McCormick
and
Horace McCormick Sr.

Thank you for letting me play with water long enough
to get comfortable with my reflection.

POEMS

Sound of Color

Three Sisters Swamp
and the Black River

Sampson County, NC

Three sisters stand in swampy lake.
Slave shadows hide in river's wake.
Master's dogs cannot find us here.
God's oldest woods most men forsake.

Ghostly hair is their mossy fear.
Blowing all night, no Whites come near.
Should my dark fate be your concern—
Cypress sisters who show no tear?

Swamp cools my skin where whippings burn.
While master prays for my return,
I pray in mud, sometimes black snow,
That none my hiding place will learn.

Brand on my back, so others know.
In rooty water dreams I sow.
Three Sisters Swamp, your hips run deep.
Callused hands have no coin to throw.

Three Sister's Swamp, my shallow sleep.
Three Sister's Swamp, my wish you keep.
Black River girls don't kiss and tell.
Three Sisters Swamp, black wishing well.

Three Sisters Swamp and the Black River in Sampson County, North Carolina, are home to three of the oldest trees in the world, known as The Three Sisters. The trees are believed to be over three thousand years old.

A Thousand Throat Songs

Mountains look over the valley like atheists
as Beijing's state police raid the Tibetan village below.
Himalayas cower to religious cleansing.
These good white fences once confined
Chinese to their own great walls.

Police force the monks to fornicate with
Buddhists nuns. They watch and masturbate
on their own dark shadows.

Chinese throw a torch into monasteries
atop smaller mountains. They burn and pop
violently in the night.

Burgundy robes sit in the lotus position and pray
for the souls and second lives of the arsonists.

Two young nuns burn juniper incense
to purify air after the Chinese leave.

Nuns pray for the Dalai Lama while his photo
dances in flame's reflection like a three-dimensional
baseball card.

In a cellar beneath Shekar, twelve monks with
separated shoulders hang by their wrists from
the ceiling of a torture chamber. They are displayed
and dispersed in even rows like curing factory meat.

In the darkness, butter candles dance like fireflies,
signaling the world with the focus
of a thousand monks singing a throat song.

James Byrd

Sound you hear is steady shrill
of nocturnal insects vibrating Texas
nightscape with paranoia, anxiety.

He frantically runs down hot paved road,
zig-zagging like a plastic running back
on an old electric football game.

Headlights from truck behind him
bear down and illuminate the moment.

James sprints like a runaway from the
angry roar of a souped-up truck. The lights
cast a shadow more significant than his life
to the drivers of the vehicle.

Headlights suck him into mouth of truck.
He is still alive. Men tie his hands together with
a twenty-foot rope. Rope tied to back bumper now.
Sound of ignition drops him to knees to pray.

A loud high school football game on the other
side of the pine trees ends on a Hail Mary.
Team huddles in the end zone to thank God
for the last second touchdown. They carry
the young running back off field.

Tomorrow someone's going to get his picture in
newspaper and be remembered.

Difference

The color black is different.
Even to Black, black is different.

Formal, exotic,
powerful, vulnerable.

Black is the most ambiguous difference.

Provokes violence like religion
Isolation like language
Fear like fire
Love like birth.

Black is the most emotional difference.

Sense black.
Hear, smell, taste, feel black.

Black is the most visible difference.

Black rules physics
Perfect emitter
Perfect absorber—nothing takes heat like black.
A hole in the universe.
Black bends space and time.

Nothing moves like the speed of black.

Black next to any color
Creates illusion of scarcity.
Never enough canvas for black.

Add a drop of black to any color
And it becomes Black.

The rule of zero rules—
Anything multiplied by black is Black,
President or princess.

Silently provocative.
More erotic than sex.
Black is different.

Black is an experiential difference.

Boat People

His brother uses fingers to write
on his parched back. A name in dry
white streaks of saltwater. They bounce
along in the wake and occasional swell
of South China Sea.

His eyes reddened fire against
burned yellow skin.
His sisters stare down path
of cargo ships sailing
through commercial lanes.
Invisible boat people wonder
if they will be welcomed
aboard or run over.

By night, he shivers against blind
fear and huddled optimism
of his family's wet skin.
He stares into dark horizon.
Knows nothing of nautical
secrets or astronomy
but much about the
beauty of a calm sea
below a starful night—
hope it brings in things
not witnessed.

He still knows more of death than life,
more of hunger than food.

As the sun rises, he wonders
if any foreign shores will embrace
them and how wide these beaches
might open arms if the hands in
their pockets were white on both sides
and their roots European.

Trumpet Player

Notices no one as he enters
The Wicked Smile.
Here to analyze self.
Serve up soul in a jazz
man's jambalaya. A musical
sacrifice for the devil he can't control.
Plays for no one but himself.

Music, the only tamable part of his life.
Turns himself inside out to express.
His play is a man's search for meaning
to understand why he is out of control
when his fingers stop moving
and his instrument waits anxiously
at his waist like a gun.

The right note and you let him in.
Dreams you drown in are wading pools
to him. His familiar waters run deep
and swell like a sea of water spouts.
He trumpets deceptively, like rising tidewater,
in and out of you. He pulls on your juices
like a full, blood-red moon.

When he plays, the earth
sits in his palm, calm, small
and occasionally blue like a
black sea. He uses you.
Your emotions fuel his music.
Instrument slave to feelings.
Callused fingers fight to sprint with mind.

Cry, laugh, get angry with his hands.
His face nothing but a stoic nightscape,
background of his life. Window to his soul
are in nerves of fingertips.
You listen and wonder if there is any such
meaning or control in your own life.

When he plays, sound breaks you
like a wild horse. Eminently, he
rides deep into your body, bareback,
black, and trumpeting.

Water Boy

A painting by Thomas Hart Benton 1946

Young Black sharecropper sits near
fields of collards and butter beans.
Wide-brim straw hat rests above ears
and brow to catch sweat and salt.
Extremities and eyes are limp with
satisfaction and exhaustion.

Red plaid shirt and worn blue jeans flow and lay
with body like many streams coming together.
His head is bowed and peaceful.
Body sits high in chair like a triple scoop of chocolate
ice cream on a small cone in the sun before it starts
to melt and drip onto bare feet.
He lifts head from prayer after thanking
God for providing good work and colorless water
to carry to his family in the field.

Black Water
Flint, Michigan 2015

It is still a **colored only** fountain
but now it is in her kitchen
so her children and mother
can die of the same brain-eating
poison you made her grandparents
drink and think sixty years ago
from a colored fountain when they had
no running water in the same
South you criticized for being
Not Like You, but
racists and violent when they
used clean water from a
high-pressure hose to press
courageous minds and mouths against
brick walls while German Shepherds
chewed the muscle in their thighs until teeth hit bone.

Immigrants

The fly in her eye senses death.
She has a newborn in her arms
who cannot blink the fly away.
There is intimacy, even here.

In the evening, yellow relief
packages fall like sunspots.
Orphans eat, blink with life.
Flies move along and seek death
in less prosperous places.

Children begin playing soccer with trash
under a bridge until the cold desert night falls,
when they must look for any person
willing to share a blanket and become family.

Les Invalids Part I

Soldier makes eye contact with Nazis
after nearly drowning on Normandy Beach.

He lives to march down the Champs Elysees.
His look is foreign to French women
who celebrate freedom and the sight
of happy, colorful, young men in Paris.

He will look at Southerners
differently after knowing these women.
He returns to Carolina unafraid
to make eye contact.

Les Invalids Part II

He is in college in Eastern North
Carolina. He walks into a French
professor's office.
Layers of ungraded papers
hang off the edges of a maple
roll-top desk. Old books are stacked
on floor like collapsed buildings.

He thinks about his uncle in Normandy.
Other books line ledges and
rest on a couch against the wall.
A window opens outward.
He sees boys playing lacrosse in snow.

There is a picture of his family standing near
the Seine, another in a flower garden
at Les Invalids, a hospice for dismembered
soldiers who fought and looted foreign
shores with Napoleon.

Professor stares into student's dark face.
The student drops eyes to floor to introduce himself.
Professor tells student, "Lift your head.
Never be afraid to make eye contact."

Negro League

Pickled pig's feet and boiled green peanuts.
Only game where soul food was as much
of the game as players. These are last days
of Sixties. A man plays golf on the moon while
we wage war in swampy fields of rice.

On this field nothing but trash-talking dreams,
team clowns, and the best baseball a Negro can buy.
My daddy brought me here to get his mind
off my brother standing for mail call today
not knowing that his Mohawk will
crash tomorrow and he and the pilot
will sprint across a foreign field for their lives.

Players hit home runs across pasture fences
built to keep cows out of the game.
Shutouts pitched on the same field
where wild cotton blooms as a reminder.
Old framed slave houses with rusted tin roofs
sag behind left field. Dented Coke signs decorate
abandoned tobacco barns. Men too old for the war
pass around whiskey in Dixie cups, talk about
how great Negro league was before integration.

Boy listens while standing under bleachers
with another six-year-old. They wait to hear the
perfect crack of a bat to bring fans to their feet
and them loose change to buy another bag
of those delicious boiled green peanuts.

Words to the Rodney King Video

A silent movie in Los Angeles 1991

Nigga'
Nigga'
Nigga'

Nigga'
Nigga'
Nigga'

Nigga'
Nigga'
Nigga'

Nigga'
Nigga'
Nigga'

Mama!
Jesus!
God!
Don't let'm kill me.

French-African Ice Skater
Surya Bonaly

In Atlanta they watched you skate like a song
at the world championships.
Sweet, smooth, sharp, and flawless
like a perfect body of water
while other skaters kissed the ice.

A journalist asked you
how you felt about second place
after a perfect performance.

"I'm used to it," you said.

Dinner with a Dutch Family

They talk about sailing, classical music,
European cars.

(Privately they think about my color while
peeling skin off slow-baked chicken.)

She smiles as he talks about an old man's travels–
Hong Kong, Malaysia, New Delhi.
With listening eyes, I daydream
about Dutch slave ships,
the Barracoons, and the Brookes Maps,
the feel of their daughter's hair
falling around my face in the dark,
the familiar collision of our complexions,
her waist between my palms, her warm whispers
and wet tongue in my ear telling me what to do.

The Barracoons were fortresses or slave castles used to temporarily hold Black cargo until ships arrived from Europe to carry them to America.

The Brookes Maps, created in England, were detailed instructions on how to tightly pack over 400 slaves "cheek by jowl" into the hull of ships with only inches between them and a few feet of headroom. The captives were stacked from bow to stern, floor to ceiling on shelves in layers like spoons. The circulation of the map across Europe and America swayed public opinion against the inhumanity of the Regulated Trans-Atlantic Slave Trade.

Layered Clothing

winter 1976

No heat in our mother's home.
Military officers gave
her old brown t-shirts
and worn wool army blankets
after cleaning their quarters.

At night cold finds
its way through door seams and
floor boards, weak window seals,
and nails loosened in attic
from a tornado.

Inhale drafts of painful cold.

In bed now, head under covers.
Breath thaws hands.
Body kept warm from the goodwill
of a green blanket
and soldiers' layered clothing.

Winter on the Outer Banks
Ocracoke Island 1984

Wind, sand, and water play a snare drum
against their tight tent. His first trip to
Ocracoke is with an older friend,
who calls himself Ventura Augusto Cuello.
Something about his name is worth saying.
He is from the Dominican Republic,
a Mason Dixon line from Haiti.

He looks at Cuello and does not understand
how people separated by an imaginary
line in the sand can be so much lighter on one side.
But he is young and has not learned as much
as he will about the sun and men,
and the freedom God gives both
to make such meaning of another's color.

He and Cuello pack their gear, firewood,
and a short story—"Hills Like White Elephants"—
and move out of cold ocean gusts and tidewater
and deeper into the Outer Banks.

Return to Hatteras Island
Summer 1999

He is on Hatteras Island with his eight-year-old son.
They watch men prepare to move the lighthouse
slowly away from beach to safer land,
closer to the sound side of the island.

Winters on the Outer Banks weaken
her walls like bones of old women.
Man and boy wish to sit here for thirty years,
the time men say it would take the lighthouse
to be consumed by sea.

He thinks about his old friend,
Ventura Augusto Cuello,
and Haiti, the cursed side of his island,
where refugees cling to boats
like a million black ants on a white
sugar cube. Inevitably, some fall off
to experience an insignificant death
by drowning, only because of color.

Cape Fear

In Cumberland County stands
a blood-red brick building
called the Market House.
A large bell sways on its yoke in the tower
and hammers the clapper.

Families herded here for auction with
palm oil on their hair and skin to hide
sores, beatings, and bruises.
Cold, sold, separated human livestock,
bartered for pigs, tobacco, and sacks of beans.

Some to work cotton and collards,
others taken to the lower Cape Fear
to work the mud and sluice gates for rice.

Plantation owners ride horses around
Market circle and dizzy the frightened
slaves who stand in tattered rags, cold, waiting,
wondering if White men are cannibals.

Married men wish for a buck,
maybe a virgin to breed or bed.
An interested buyer dismounts
to ask a chained child to show her teeth
and body like a broodmare.
Wives watch and debate if these beings
have souls.

Indians of the Lumber River stare at the
spectacle and discuss the savagery of the event.
They know the imminence of their own
relationship with European immigrants.

For the Lumbee, extinction
is a better fate than slavery
as long as they are with their ancestors
and the buffalo—known only from stories that
blew across the Smokey Mountains from far away.

A Woman Asks His Color

A smiling young woman from Africa asks
a dark Black man, "What is your color?"
as if she doesn't know. She is Moroccan.
She walks away when he gives his answer.
This is the Rhone Valley in rural France.
Village lies below hills massive like herds of whales.
Silent volcanos filled and hardened,
covered with waves of green grass.

He stands against wire and wood fence
outlining a path leading up the small mountain.
Wire is not like any you would see
meandering miles of ranches in West Texas.

He stops along fence to admire families
who sit in beaches of tall grass eating bread,
cheese, and drinking wine from the vineyard below.

He tries to understand the Moroccan woman's question.
He said he is Black and American before she walked away.
He continued up the volcano, meeting himself
each step of his metamorphic journey.

Silent Sam

An old, old secret lies on a hill
in woods where periwinkle grows
as students topple Silent Sam
before asking what he knows.

A secret lies along that hill
and cascades down its sides,
as students topple Silent Sam
before asking what he hides.

Walnut, cedar, a holly tree,
do quiet work to conceal
as students topple Silent Sam,
dark secret must not reveal.

Buried, Black, dark and deep
on the highest point in town
as students topple Silent Sam
and the secret under the ground.

Look behind the plantation house
where the Barbee family rose
as students topple Silent Sam
and the secret that he knows.

Walk behind Dubose House
to find out what he knows
about two hundred unmarked stones
where the lavender flower blows.

Follow bricks to wood and flower
and take a deep, free breath,
for there you will stand
on slaves freed by their death.

The resilient periwinkle was used by slaves to mark their graves and served as the perfect symbol of their endurance and legacy. The Barbee Family Cemetery, located on the UNC Chapel Hill property, may be the oldest slave cemetery in the country. The slaves buried there built the oldest public university in the country. The cemetery has been there for over 300 years and kept secret by the business school leadership to avoid controversy over its prized five-star Rizzo Conference Center, Hotel, Swimming Pool expanding on the same hilltop.

Moments

Picking Strawberries

I remember picking
strawberries in the country
with Mom. We took a long dirt road
to a strawberry patch
in Harnett County near Buffalo Lakes.
She knew what to do, where to go,
which rows and patches
to stay away from.
We gathered our white
buckets and walked toward
thick, sunbaked fields
of berries.

I followed her in a parallel row,
stayed a few steps behind,
the way I did for thirty-five
years. She strutted down
dusty rows and passed hundreds
of leafy patches with
beautiful, heart-red sweet
peeking at me from under
green cover. She reminded me
to break them above the stem.
She was a farmer's child.
We wore wide-brimmed hats
and cool white t-shirts.

We washed the berries and ate
them plain and clean at her kitchen
table until our lips and hearts were red,
full, and happy with each other.

Emergency Room

Lying on bed,
oxygen.
Hip, sternum,
ribs broken.
Leg distorted.
Face a big,
bruised strawberry.

She is known here.
Doctor recognizes
name on chart.
Too old to drive.
Another seizure
behind the wheel.
This time he will take
the keys. Ten years
too late.

He rubs hands
across her face into her
hair. She cannot see.
In and out of consciousness,
but knows by feel this
is her baby coming to hold
her again, and again,
until she is able to go with him
into the country to pick
strawberries once more.

Baseball

Brother enters the room.
Daddy watches a baseball game.
Maybe Hank Arron is about to
hit his homerun, break Babe's record.
Door is almost closed.
From the hallway, boy peeks
to see Hank swing.

Brother stands in front
of Daddy—he sits on edge
of the bed like a boy,
head down, listens to
brother become a man.

He wants to quit drinking.
He wants to come home at night.

Raise my brother,
love my mother,
brother tells him.

Mom listens while staring out
the window above an empty sink
in the kitchen. Daddy thinks about gin
hiding behind old hats in the living room
closet and the bootlegger two
houses down. While my brother talks,
Daddy sweats his uncontrollable desires.

Hank swings.
My brother becomes a man,
and a young Black boy has a hero.

Snowbird

Bicentennial summer 1976, a fifteen-year-old boy in backyard
chain link fence plays with a Saint Bernard. Father appears.
Reaches over metal barbs to touch his happy, red dog.
Dad makes eye contact with boy. She was his dog too,
when he lived there. Boy has not seen him since winter, two
years ago.

(December, 1974, a blizzard outside,
cold stands firm like mountains.
Darkness falls early through a snowy curtain as his
father staggers toward home from bootlegger's bar stool.

Boy begins to unpack a silver Christmas tree from
a box in the attic. He pauses to hear a preacher's knock.
He wears black—clothes, hat, and jacket.
Preacher is also Black. When boy opens door, preacher stands
on porch like death.
Full snowbirds abandon a bare hickory tree behind
him when he speaks or collects the rent. Preacher tells
boy his father is lying in the snow half mile away.

The boy and the big dog begin the walk in dark, white
nightscape to gather father.

Snowbirds reappear on limbs of leafless trees.
A lone bird perches on an old pear tree that sits
in a clearing. It stares at father who
wondered off street into the clearing
bordered by groves of bare plum orchards.
He has drifted too many times, too far away, to come
home again. He lies in snow, a few yards from
where preacher last saw him.

Dog sniffs him and recognizes gin and unfiltered
camels. She licks his chapped face warm.
Boy gathers small man to feet like shaking out heavy wet
laundry. His clothes have life again as he walks against
boy like a wounded soldier. Boy will put him to bed and
decorate the Christmas tree before father awakens.)

Father walks into yard on this sober summer morning
for visitation. He says hello. Dog greets him happily,
unconditionally, as boy will, without barbed fences between
them.

Deep Creek

He said it was good that I took him fishing
the day his mother's body
was lowered into Deep Creek.

He brings me a 1935 pistol from his bedroom.
It was a luger taken from a Nazi soldier
with art stolen from Bavarian caves.
He tells me Audie Murphy kept
a gun under his pillow too.

In his backyard, we clear land,
burn cedar branches soaked in gasoline.
Black faces shine in fiery shadows.
He wants to burn a century old barn
at the edge of the woods.
I ask him to spare the barn.

We talk about Boston, Prince Hall,
and secrets of Black Masonry
during the Revolutionary War.
A 1949 red Dodge War Wagon
sits on the opposite side of fire.
He called me when his wife tried
to run him over with the antique.
She said he was cheating,
and she didn't want to mess up
her new car.

In the morning we left his house, walking
through thick mud to another funeral.
He reminded me why people from
Deep Creek wear boots and of the
tornado we survived driving across
this hilltop thirty years ago.

Elevator Ride

A mother leaves hospital in wheel chair,
holding flowers to chest, waving
at nurses with her free hand.
She is in a parade or a beauty pageant.
She tells son that she gave birth to
him in this building.

In her lap is a small bucket
of hospital toothpaste, paper cups,
mouthwash, and other things she
believes the hospital was nice enough
to give her. She was raised in the
depression.

Nurses who know her say "goodbye and
try not to come back here, but we
love you." She smiles with the grace
of a thousand queens.

She reminds son that this is the hospital
that would not take her first child,
who died from meningitis during segregation.

Son wheels her into the elevator.
An old man enters behind them
pushing his IV pole.
Doctors removed his voice
and left him to listen to the world.

An old woman and her daughter enter
on next floor. Daughter combs her

mother's hair with her fingers as
mother forces a smile to one side of
face against the gravity of a stroke.
Doors close again—they descend.

Doors open to a woman who wheels
her exhausted but smiling daughter
into elevator. Her daughter carries a new
baby girl wrapped in a yellow blanket.

Doors close. Open to lobby and a new father.
He carries roses and puppy's breath,
smiles at his wife and new daughter
wrapped in sunlight and optimism.

Son wheels mother onto blue carpet,
remembering all the beautiful things that have
happened between the two of them
in the hospital.

Old Black Woman Knows

Scrubbing floors
Cleaning toilets
On her knees
For her children.
Old Black woman knows God.

Sifting through soot
And ashes in a burned Black church
On her knees
Praying for other saints.
That old woman knows God.

Begging a frustrated man to quit
Beating, lying, cheating
On her knees
By the side of her father.
That old woman knows God.

By the side of the road
By the side of her children
On her knees
By the side of her bed.
Old Black woman knows God.

Moonlight Cotton Fields

Orange moon is three-quarters waxing
on the Cape Fear River in Harnett County.
Over the hood of the truck, he sees a cotton field,
full bloom in harvest light. A robin scoops a beak
of white for a nest.

He hears a choir rehearsing in a church nearby.

He left his second wife on this moon.
They were together only weeks
before he learned she was bipolar.
It was he who asked for the marriage to end.
She was a flooding night river,
flowing toward and away in the same hour.

She loved and hated him with the tide.
Loved him for loving her.
Hated him for loving his mother.
Loved him for crying on the porch in rain
the day her family drove her away
with a Bible in her lap.

She hated herself for being ill.
He had a son to raise—from his first wife
who made him leave.
She wanted another.
He let the river move him to new places,
her to deeper water.

The women in church sing through stain glass.
He stands in moonlight glowing on cotton,
unable to escape guilt and the Word of church folk.

Black Harley Rider
South Carolina 1999

Black Harley rider cruises easy
through upstate of South Carolina
near Echo Valley. Civil War bullets
and belt buckles are for sale in a local
store near the foothills.

Confederate flags cover the building
like cheap wallpaper. He can still hear
soft sounds of slurs and whispers from
rebel ghosts and bully statues.

He roars through back road mountain
passes, against trout streams, old Klan
country, loud and defiant, wearing an
American flag bandana, a pack of unfiltered
camels rolled into t-shirt sleeve, fingertips
cut from gloves.

He continues ride toward state capitol,
blasting songs by Prince—"Thieves in the Temple,"
"Controversy," and "Let's Go Crazy."
The Confederate flag waves at him in hard wind
and makes percussion-like sounds as if
shouting expletives to anyone thinking
about removing it.

The ocean rises to greet him as he pulls into
Myrtle Beach. He thunders through narrow
corridors of tourist and voyeurs. Calm blue

sea clashes against sound of brash tailpipes
under black leather chaps.

Black rider takes his helmet off to feel freedom,
daring the deep-rooted, foolish rebellion of
South Carolina.

Blue Socks and Brown Shoes

Harrisonburg, VA 1994

Some days
he finds himself
sitting there on the edge
of the bed,

frozen,

half dressed,
one leg in his black pants,
one blue sock on

staring at the other pillow,
wondering how he lost her
and which foot to put his
left brown shoe on.

Sea Rations

The night is long.
He lies on a twin bed
wet with sticky, southern humidity
soaked into his sheets.

He hears a bark
at a distant owl. These
are dog days of summer,
and it is too hot to sleep.

He feels the restlessness of hunger.
Hears sounds coming from mother's
bedroom. He peeks through and sees
an old jewelry box in the mirror.
She sits on a squeaky
red bar stool rolling her hair.

Inside the box are his father's old watches,
frozen dates and time,
old cuff links, tie pins,
and rings with missing stones.
The only things she has left of him.

He takes another look into a nearly
empty cupboard. He finds an old can
of sea rations given to his mother
for cleaning the bathroom of a paratrooper
who knew they were hungry.

House on Willow Street

His house is on the Tar River in Greenville,
North Carolina. This house has no heat, furniture,
or women.

A mattress is on the floor.
He cannot afford tables, blankets, or pillows.
He dreams of what he would do if he should
ever own a pillow.

On cold nights, he covers himself
with piles of clean clothes.
Lights are off and a street lamp
illuminates the room. He has no curtains or other
window dressings. He listens to an old soul album on a
record player as he moves around to get comfortable
under layers of jeans and soft towels.

Morning, he moves clothes around in shape
of a table to rest a breakfast plate. After eating,
he adjusts pile of clothes like Legos and builds
a desk to study medieval literature.

In a few hours, he will wear the legs of his desk to a physics
class. In the evening, he will push clothes against the wall
to rest his back while he eats fish caught for dinner
on the river where he lives.

After dinner, he will write a poem about life in his simple
house to remind himself, should he ever own a pillow,
he will lay his head on it in the grass next to the river
behind the little house on Willow Street.

A Party Downstairs

Put son to bed.
Pray, hug, I love you, Dad.

Phone sleeps on the kitchen table.
Pray, hug, I love you, Dad.

Friends have a party downstairs.
Pray, hug I love you, Dad.

Hear beautiful voices of women.
Pray, hug, I love you, Dad.

Their voices knock on neighbor's door.
Pray, hug, I love you, Dad.

Laughter answers and closes the door.
Pray, hug, I love you, Dad.

Lie down on bed alone,
listen to the vibrations
of music and voices below.
Pray, hug, I love you, Dad.

Mirror Talk

To hold hand that slapped you,
to shake hand that choked you,
to fight him or to hug him,
to love her or to leave her,
when we come face-to-face,
pray the mirror smiles.

Field of Flowers

Daddy,

you should have
lived long enough
to see your children
love their little boys
like every day is
a new butterfly

and time is
an infinite field of flowers.

Reading Lesson for an Abandoned Father and Son

See daddy wash my butt.
See daddy praise my butt.

See daddy cook my food.
See daddy burn my food.
See daddy eat my food.

See daddy pray for me.
See daddy work for me.
See daddy dream for me.

See daddy hold my hand.
See daddy sing me sleep.
See daddy hug me tight.

See daddy learn with me.
See daddy laugh with me.
See daddy cry with me.

See daddy love me.
See daddy love me.
See daddy love me.

Run mama.
See mama run.

Searching for Seashells
in the Family Room

Grandchildren watch him take shoes
off in family room to search for seashells.

He cannot remember why teapots
whistle, what color to call clear sky.
He forgot the name of beautiful white
puffy things that sail above the horizon.

He cannot remember his dog's name or to light
the cigarette. He does not know what to do
about the candles on his cake when
family stops singing happy birthday.

His youngest daughter has become his childhood
cat. He wonders if flower petals are edible
and if coins on the living room floor are seashells.

Thunder Snow

Son asleep in child seat
between luggage and
stuffed animals.
He holds a box of
French fries upside
down. A neat stack
on floor beneath his
feet like timber.

Another headlight. Blinding.
Grip the wheel, head down,
continue up mountain
out of the Valley.

Snow becomes heavy
and wet. Fog waits to
ambush at summit.
Curtain of snow closing
hope of getting home for
Christmas. Scores of stranded
travelers wait
near Walton's Mountain.

Babies sleep in backseats.
We pass more cars spun around
backwards, folks helpless and huddling
to stay warm. Do not run out of gas.
Do not kill battery.

Thunder snow cracks,
explodes, roars through
mountain pass like Civil War artillery.

Braking will cause slide and helplessness.
Darkness, fog thicker.
Nerves reach into back for cold
fries on floor. At scenic view,
we see town below, sitting like a
model train village.

Start down mountain
in low gear looking for
lights of Charlottesville.

Canoeing

They tighten life jackets
and launch a long canoe.
She sits at bow facing her son.
He returns from summer visitation.

He sits in back facing his son.
He too returns from summer visitation.

Our oars are in water.
Canoe glides effortlessly across stillness.

He sees a large fallen tree across lake,
his azimuth. Their boys turn
face to face and smile.
She smiles over them at him.

Canoe is near the fallen tree.
They stare silently at branches
peeking above surface like periscopes.

In middle of lake, she is happy again
but worries about being a good mother
for her son, who misses his father and
sometimes says he wants to live with him.

They sit a while to watch a patient
man catch fish.

They have many differences—
countries, accents, colors, cultures,
and still she removes her life jacket.

They canoe into more open water,
safe from the world and summer visitation.

And he thinks about removing his vest
and returning her physical affection.

A Night in Mexico

Her aunt is a small passionate woman
who fears only God and earthquakes.
She offers them the same room
but not the same bed.

Hear a train grinding through sweating night.
Feel steel wheels ride bones
like a small terremoto.
Black mass screams through stucco,
vibrates his white hammock.

House welcomes dark ghost
each midnight like a familiar body
in darkness. Feel the rhythm and bump
of each car hitting the same spot between rails.

Train passes.
He reaches out to hold the hand of the woman
lying in the bed near his swing.

The open window talks back to the train
in a nervous, high-pitched rattle.
Her fingers play soft piano on his palm.
Nothing breaks her focus on simple love.
Not blinding train in the bedroom window
nor the bellow of its throaty whistle.

He inhales scent of mango from the window's breath.
The rush of the train lifts him from hammock
and into the blankets of the Mexican woman
who carefully holds his heart in her hands.

The Little Bedroom

She takes him to her little bedroom
in the thick mix of Mexico City.
A rooster crows to Latin music at sunrise.
An uncovered light bulb hangs by black wire
and casts shadows to her bed.

Her room is seven feet long, seven feet wide.
A nice place to get to know yourself
in a city of thirty-four million.

Walls are concrete block, bare and safe.
Books rest on wood shelf.
She reads Victor Hugo, Arthur Rimbaud.
Les Misérables leans against *The Drunken Boat*.

A clean twin bed asleep on dusty floor.
A small window is face-to-face
with a neighbor's pane.
Red flowers happily climb white stucco walls.

Thirty-four years she lived here with parents
as Mexican women do until married.
Yesterday she said yes.
Her mother hugged them
and wept while cleaning the memory
of her daughter's little room for the last time.

Revival

In no-where North Carolina,
a small town summer revival
tent blooms in parking lot
of an abandoned gas station
where weeds grow between
cracked concrete.

Most nights dealers and prostitutes
work this lot like a vegetable and
fruit stand. Tonight, shiny gray
metal chairs are neatly placed on
both sides of the tent to form an aisle.

Maybe a wife will come back home
to a man in the tent who wears uneven brown
shoes. He cries with two small girls
wearing purple dresses with yellow daisies.

He hears the shake of tambourines.
People pour into canvas church,
clapping and curious.

Preacher is doing his dance.
Hands are in the air. Someone's
speaking in tongues, another about
to get happy, while a hooker is paid
in sight across street.

Families can hear the Word and invitation
through hot living room windows.
Some turn up volume on a radio.
Another family closes windows.

A teenage girl and boyfriend walk
into tent, looking for something to believe.
Preacher feels good. Plate is heavy.
Maybe someone will be blessed
with a miracle, get saved,
or have the baby.

In a week, preacher leaves,
tent down, chairs folded,
tambourines quiet.

The vegetable stand is back
and open for business, and a
hopeful mother comes home
to uneven brown shoes and
purple dresses with yellow daisies.

Departures

Cherry Snow Cones
Kosovo 1993

Sound of frostbitten children,
whimpering like new puppies,
provides cadence for the march.
They walk through night to avoid
soldier patrols as homes burn
in wintered countryside.

Blood from removed saints and soldiers
stains the snowy path like cherry snow cones.
A captured boy in prison camp
stares through fresh barbed wire at the walkers.
He wants a touch from someone free.

Families walk through smell of death,
search for refuge, some for easier death.
They trod by shallow graves on the side of the road.
Reason battles with instinct over choice to survive.

Children on the march hold hands
of women who were once someone's mother.
Each day someone dies or disappears,
while another gives birth in the same pile
of wet leaves in the woods.

At nautical twilight, see a friendly devil's cross
hunt tanks on hilltops.
A silent surface-to-air missile streaks
into Kosovo sky, collides with cross.
A faithful old man on the march
makes a wish as if the flash were a falling star.

The Lamb – Jamal Kashoggi
Saudi journalist butchered in the Turkish Consulate

The Cherokee way to dress out a lamb begins with prayer.
The tribe honors the lamb throughout her short life.
She is given the same heart-felt respect as the
mysterious buffalo.

Native Americans know and recognize the lamb
for courage, innocence, and gentleness
as playmate with the tribe's children.
A lamb is often the first animal native children touch.
Cherokee value the lamb for the curiosity she creates
in toddlers, the first step toward living without fear
of differences.

In honor of the lamb's sacrifice, her dressing out
is respected as a religious ritual, a right-of-passage
for providing nourishment to the tribe.
Muslims, much like Cherokee, would not
expect their home to be known as an abattoir
that does not respect the religious customs
required in the slaughter of a lamb.

Jamal's fiancée, Hatice Cengiz, waited outside
the Turkish consulate wearing purple and black,
happily, innocently waiting for the journalist to walk out,
to see his smile on round face, hear his laughter
and feel his hands on the documents that would
have finalized their marriage.

Khashoggi was sacrificed without prayer
because he told the truth about the slaughter

of Yemeni children and fought for rights of Saudi women
to speak to men without beating or butchery.
He is a martyr that produces more courageous
lambs even after a death without rights or rituals.

Paperboy – Departure to Vietnam

Fayetteville, NC 1969

My brother sits on couch,
wears a white t-shirt, khakis,
and a shaved head. Silver dog
tags around his neck.
He is eighteen or nineteen.
I am five.

My mother and sisters are here.
We laugh some. He tickles me.
I know he jumps from airplanes.
We watched clouds spit hundreds
of flowering paratroopers from the sky
last summer at Fort Bragg.

My mother watches a clock in a curio.
It sits next to a bronze statue of RFK
and a wooden black fist—
a reminder of last year's Olympics
in Mexico City, and RFK and MLK's
assassinations.

We do not have a telephone or car.
A taxi arrives and sits quietly
on dirt road in front of our
stucco duplex. It is Daddy and Mr. Note
to take brother to the train station
to answer the call of the draft.

My sister runs into her room, closes door.
I can hear her crying on the bed. I press against
the screen door and watch brother

get into back seat. The yellow light
on the taxi roof fades as car disappears
down our narrow dirt road.

Brother left me an old leather football
and his dog. I grab a sheet from his bed,
tie it like a parachute. I jump off front porch
and yell "Airborne" with the football in my hand,
pretending I am my brother
as my dog runs away after the taxi.

My mother looks at his picture in the curio and
remembers when he was just a paperboy.

Tiananmen Square

Glass ponds and fragile flower gardens
bordered by non-negotiable great walls,
heavenly gates, illusions of peace.
Once home to imperial families,
now Mongols, Manchus, and Turkics.

Students preparing Molotov cocktails
wait for roar of Army to parade into
their rebellious intellect. Soon metal
rhythm of tracked vehicles vibrate
this emotional square into Rubik's Cube.

Protesting students beckon imminent
confrontation in the square. Matador taunts
tanks strong enough to resist mortars and
minefields but vulnerable to one free man's
impermeable will to hold his ground.

Return from Vietnam

I am seven years old and
the taxi returns.
We have a telephone now.
There is a man on the moon
and a new president.

A larger man climbs out of the taxi.
He carries duffle bags.
He turns toward the house,
dog tags safely at his chest.
I see my brother's face resting
comfortably under a soldier's hat.

I run into my room, grab the old leather
football and my Joe Namath helmet to let
him know that I am ready to
be his brother again,
hoping he will forgive me for
losing his dog.

Platoon Leader

He smells crude oil boiling in Middle Eastern pit like
hot molasses. He feels the simmer of panic at sight
of another man's boots with no one left to walk them.
He hears the womp, womp, womp of a military
helicopter flying nap of the earth behind
the wailing echoes of an Islamic chant.

He knows the silly stuttering of an Israeli machine gun
in Bethlehem, the raining of Palestinian rocks
from rooftops on tracked vehicles made in Detroit.
He hears the roar and squeak they talk
down ancient cobblestone roads stained with diesel fuel.

He sees his heartbeat against dog tags as fear sits next
to him in a foxhole like an imaginary friend
waiting for him to make eye contact. He tastes
chalkiness of a soldier's unbrushed teeth, bland grit
of desert in his mouth, saltiness of dry blood from licking
cracked lips in a place where there are no Sundays.

It makes him doubt that Jesus was born in this part of the
world.

He was inspired to service after looking at the famous
photograph of naked Vietnamese girl,
crying in street, clothes blown off, burns rinsed
clean by rainwater and tears, as she sprints
barefoot on a wet road for a hug from an elusive God.

Measurement – A Son Comes Home

He touches face on mother's
bathroom mirror after returning home.
Feels changes this time,
like finishing a marathon after the crowd
has gone home—no tape, no applause.
First time he has seen crow's feet
at the corners of tired eyes. Bright lights
and sweat accent a spot of gray hair
on a nearly shaved head.

He measures himself against childhood notches
cut into the wall, wonders why he never
got as tall as he thought he would
and if he is still the same reflection
on mother's mirror.

Dead Captain's House

Optimism enters a house with a realtor.
House is one year old and alone.
Back porch with white columns overlooks a pond.
This is where he gave her the ring and told her
he would come back. The buyer asks the agent
if this was a soldier's house.

The house answers his question with her solemn stare.
This is a military community and many soldiers are at war.
She takes the buyer into the kitchen to show him the fine
oak above blue granite surfaces and the hand crafted
fixtures the young officer added to surprise his fiancée.

She brings attention to shiny hardwood floors on which
they practiced ballroom dancing before his orders.
The agent points to the crystal chandelier that bumped his
head after the third glass of Chilean merlot on their
last night before his deployment.

The buyer's eyes drifted upward to the double tray
bedroom ceiling the couple admired when lying in bed
on Sunday mornings, day-dreaming about life in
the new home. The agent lowers the buyer's eyes to the
porcelain floor where the captain's fiancée wore his wool
army socks on cold winter mornings.

The buyer admires the wood fireplace in a limestone frame.
His fiancée drew this on paper when they began planning
for a home, children, and a normal life after his service.

Two Soldiers' Custody Battle

You may have carried him,

but he carried both of you
with a heart of stretch marks
and purple battle scars

until his feet began to swell.

You may have carried him,
but he carried you,

without forgetting your better
days as soldiers.

Veterans Hospital

First time here, I was nauseous.
Six years now and it is easier.
This time I sit next to an old man
in a wheel chair in the pharmacy
waiting room.

His wife is tired of coming here.
Anxiety and panic make home with her.
She cannot look at the two amputees
who greet each other in the hallway.
The last time they saw each other,
they had four legs. They laugh and talk
about their new prostheses and exchange
phone numbers.

I offer her my seat so she can sit next
to her husband. She does not wish to sit
next to his wheel chair. She does not
understand why the rest of her life is
committed to taking care of someone
she used to love. She stares straight
ahead at the next number like a frightened
soldier following orders, waiting to be called.

Veteran Fishing Under a Bridge

Cars above run over invisible man
fishing between concrete pillars.
Tires make rhythm above him.

Steel structures jut perpendicular to face,
supporting the new road.
Many forgot about the old bridge
left beneath its successor.

Silver water animation bites
through a hole in foggy bottom.
He adds another to a white bucket.

When he looks at the water,
he hears no sounds,
happy now that his life is nothing
but an old bridge free of expectations.

Never again ask him to answer
the call of his last name
or to defend a bridge never worthy of crossing.

Siamese Alligators I

The shooter – Lee Boyd Malvo

Shooter examines her bare shoulders.
She is young, twenty something, drives a black convertible.
She just happens to be the woman who follows attractive legs
and short skirt out of the driver's seat.

He has her in his crosshairs from one hundred yards.
Driver admires patience in his young apprentice.
Shooter lies in prone position in the trunk.
The hourglass cutout next to trunk key hole
is large enough for the sight and barrel of his rifle.

He feels his pulse through earplugs.
He takes a deep breath, holds his breathing
long enough to take a perfect shot between heartbeats.
He examines other targets like a voyeur or slasher as if this
random act would satisfy any day's itch or most private need.

He moves the cross onto a convenience store clerk,
then to a man unloading bottled water,
back to the young woman. He squeezes the trigger
and becomes his own God.

Siamese Alligators II
The driver – John Allan Muhammad

Driver observes through rear view mirror.
He is a hyena who watches offspring learn to hunt
from a distant grove of baobab trees. He taught him how
to disconnect himself from the savagery of an explosive
death. How to kill for sport,
as insignificant as throwing carnival darts
at colored water balloons.

After all, you are only pulling a trigger. That's all.
It is not a baseball bat or an axe.

They crawl guiltlessly away,
like Siamese alligators,
until hungry again.

Life After Drowning I

Earth exhaled ocean.
Death rang the doorbell of his hotel,
ignoring the "do not disturb" signs
hanging on brass knobs.

She indiscriminately chose children to orphan
and grandmothers to have no grandchildren—
there is no word for what these women will be called.
No saint singled out for faithfulness
nor given time to collect two of anything.

He calls from a beach hotel in Southeast Asia
to say he survived the greatest
natural disaster of our time, maybe,
and that it was good that my passport had expired.

When the second wave hit, rising water swallowed
a large billboard of the King of Thailand,
drowning his image.
He was nearly God in this world
before this tsunami killed three hundred thousand people.

Near an old beach market, mothers toss
dozens of drowned infants into a pit like firewood.
Others are shoveled into the large crater
with earthmoving equipment.
A worker wearing whites and a surgical mask
sprays green disinfectant over the small bodies.

A woman finds her baby tangled in a bush.
She kisses and gives the child to a man

who puts the body into the face of an iron Caterpillar.
Yellow steel jaws drop bodies into mass grave.
Swollen and stiff, they stack like little green
plastic soldiers in a boy's toy box.

Life After Drowning II

Why can't we lie at the bottom of a weedy lake
or flow down the Mississippi 'til we meet the
crystal sea, body and soul quietly admiring the
beautiful colors of saltwater fish?

Why can't our spirits swim invisibly with a school
of seahorses or lie peacefully next to a man o' war
minding his own business for eternity
without worry of heaven?

Rhino Horn

In the shallow floodplains of Africa
a bearded, tan man stands
over an adult female rhino.
She bleeds out into mud wallow.
Her fleshy checks rise and fall
with her last labored breaths.

One boot rests on
the dry side of her fat, mud-crusted belly.
A long rifle stands
in his right hand.
Butt of weapon pressed
against her fallen shoulders.

In his left hand a useless,
superstitious trophy
raised in his honor
cut from her beautiful face
with a battery powered
construction saw.

Yale's Daughter

This started as an ordinary day,
but there is nothing ordinary
about the drowning of a man's
two-year-old daughter.

Yale is the son of a famous football player,
a self-consumed Hall of Famer.
He is not his dad's son.

I admire his beautiful baby daughter's photograph
on the desk in front of us.
He begins to tell me a story—the night of her death.

> *A young man mops wood floor of an*
> *old home, first home for his new*
> *wife and their two-year-old daughter,*
> *who became their commitment.*
> *He met his wife while she worked the counter*
> *at a convenience store in Texas.*
> *He was in graduate school.*
>
> *On the night of his toddler's last,*
> *his wife calls him into bedroom to make love.*
> *She undresses him.*
> *He undresses her.*
>
> *Their two-year-old daughter walks into the*
> *kitchen from her bedroom. She plays with*
> *the large metal bucket father uses to mop floor.*
> *Bucket is as large as she. It is full of ammonia*
> *and water. She reaches into the wheeled pail and*

folds at the waist. Her screams are muted
in thick, lung-burning liquid and heavy breathing of
her mother and father.

My wife has never forgiven me, he says,
and I have never forgiven myself.
His one-year-old son lumbers toward us.
Smile reminds us that God forgives
and makes us whole again.

The Blue Heron

Susan Smith, summer 1994

A female heron stands full
and at peace in the marsh.
She admires teeming new life
in the wetlands surrounding her
while a mother near the dock
drowns her children.

Car rolls down concrete boat ramp.
She watches vehicle drink lake.
She hears familiar screams of wet children.
Car erases into watery place.

Sound of soft wind blows cattails
on calm lake warming in sun.
She feels better now, full and free,
like the blue heron in the marsh.

She closes her eyes,
takes a deep breath,
and imagines the two men
as black as a moonless night
who drowned her baby boys

and the police who will
skate about like Jesus bugs
and water striders,
looking for two innocent men.

Church Steps of Morehead City

Seven-year-old's first funeral,
a young aunt, first person he
knows to die. In the church,
he sits between his mom and dad.

Near the front feels too close.
He begins to feel sick.
Dad walks him out of the church.
He holds hand over mouth.
People stare.

Sitting on the church porch,
they see gulls fly back streets
around this small, old shipbuilder's
town. Give him water. Unbutton shirt.
Loosen tie. He puts his head
between hands, elbows on knees,
looks down at black shoes, reminds
father that he did not cry.

Father sits quietly against his shoulder.
Son feels confused about
time and length of life with father.

Talking Lake

Toddlers play on frozen lake.
Daughter digs two inches
into ice with a sharp stick for fish
she caught and threw back last spring.

Boy and girl focus on lake's voice
as she talks to them in hums and gurgles.
Son answers in language of water.

Ice warms and snaps from new sun,
with the sound of breaking stringed
instruments, one wire at a time.

Siblings return to lake at midnight and
she welcomes them in echoes like
Northern Lights.

Breathing Lessons

Breathing isn't like riding a bike.
Sometimes you just stop doing it
because something terrible makes you forget how.

And when you remember, it's not air anymore.
It's all burning, unsure, wobbly, and you feel like
you need breathing lessons to get back on again.

The Echo Hole

A teen-ager stands in front of Dan in a dark foyer
with loaded shotgun. He aims with finger on trigger.
In eighteen seconds, someone is dead.

> *When they were little, they played on a stream*
> *dividing Black neighborhoods from White.*
> *This was before school integration.*
> *The stream is Little Cross Creek.*

> *They laughed and called White boys names*
> *that echoed back on their safe side of the body of water.*
> *They cannonballed from a rope tied to a cypress tree.*

The girl welcomes him into house. Her brother
appears from behind the door with the shotgun.
He aimed—Dan yells. The brother laughs,
tells friend the gun does not work. The laugh
vibrates the finger resting on the trigger.

He lies on his back, eyes open. Lungs begin to fill with
blood. He cannot gather enough breath to scream.
The room begins to darken.

In his last moment, he forgets about the girl and the gunshot.
He thinks about fishing the Echo Hole and the beautiful
prism-like colors on the backs of wet fish in the sunlight.

He remembers how quickly he would always try to release
fish from his hands into the cool water to breathe again.
He thought how simple things were, when they played
with their own echoes and skipped rocks at White boys
on Little Cross Creek.

Water

Creek Water

She carried an old blue bucket
with half-moon metal handle
into woods and creek.
Beautiful voices of birds
chatter in background above.

Distant sound of suburban
traffic muted by canopies of green.
Dirt path welcomes steps,
concealing a stream of
clean water rolling over rocks.

She stands her bucket on soft
bed of damp pine straw.
A dry, splintered wooden hoe rests against tree.
Hoe and bucket cast shadows of an instrument
resting against a musician's knee.

She sits on the edge of creek bed,
watches water move
over a large
white rock sitting peacefully
in cool water.

She hears nothing now but softness
of creek water flowing like
Lionel Hampton playing solo on vibes.
Hear the echo of his soft bells rolling
downstream, sanitizing rock and worry.

Launching a Dory

Horses barely broken
pull broad wooden fishing boat
through sand and sea shells,
cold as packed snow.

Captain wearing yellow waders pulls lead
horse by bridle, commands her forward,
closer to beach before tide chases moon
and fish back over edge of flat earth.

Team drags boat to sea, fighting for every inch.
Horses strain from boat's weight, herring nets,
and heavy wooden oars. Determined, sharp bow
plows sand, splits earth to greet sea.

Foam, crashing water, tingling sand
from receding waves call captain closer.
Exhausted horses are free in surf.
The dory waits for a wave.

Weathered face charges water,
hands gripped along high
gunwales. He pushes boat into
ocean's mouth.

Sea surges under vessel's chin,
uppercuts and shoves her nose
skyward, punching her hull
with knuckled whitecaps.

She battles beach
to break free from the
labor of the launch and
dangerous breakers.

Captain hurls himself into boat,
heads to a place where ocean deepens
and lies down to respect the primitive
strength, launching the dory into sea.

Lighthouse Keeper

Visions of lost ships awaken
him from small white
keeper's house with a
fragile wooden porch.
Paint peels from broken,
aged, black shutters.

Like Van Gogh's *Bedroom at Arles*,
the lighthouse keeper knows
the beauty of self-awareness.
Small unmade bed in a corner
next to a lone wooden chair
and a white bowl for bathing.

Stucco sanctuary kept warm
with black wood stove.
Candlelight and kerosene lanterns
to read by,
stars and moonlight
to see by.

A ship's horn calls
him to a lonely window
stained with saltwater
blemishes. He views
lighthouse through
cracked panes.

Beacon flashes three second
bursts of light into his life.
He enters lighthouse,

climbs black wrought iron spiral stairs
to the lantern area
to find remedy for loneliness.

Hurricane

Everyone escapes west, away from coast.
Floyd muscles his way toward the Outer Banks,
somewhere between Hatteras and Cape Fear.

Storm begins to talk.
Wind blows horizontal rain.
No one east bound but me.

This time I will make her come home with me,
stubborn old woman. I know she is afraid.
She has touched the eyewall of many hurricanes.
Hazel, Hugo, Fran, her father, and her baby sister.

She knows the furious sound of pine roots
tearing through earth,
hope hiding in static of a weak weather radio
clinched to chest.

I walk into her house without a knock.
Her luggage packed this time.
She waits for me while sitting underneath
a black velvet tiger my brother brought
home from a war forty years ago.

Detour to Princeville

a town founded by freed slaves

Cross the Tar River, enter Princeville,
a ghost town. Hurricane Floyd left no one here.

Imagine voices of Black children playing
in streets. They lick raw sticks of sweet cane.
Others sit in shade on surface roots under
maple trees, spitting watermelon seed for sport.

Old Black women on gossiping porches
snap peas. Black men cane fish under
the Tar River bridge.

Hear the screams and panic when the dam
breaks. Lives, homes, streets abandoned.
Washed away in backwater
and swollen brackish of a hurricane.

Cross the river again and stop along
the side of the road to take a photograph.
A pregnant, dark-skin child in rear view mirror.
She stares from a paneless window, a condemned
house with sagging roof.

She wonders why her grandmother did not
come home after the water broke.

Alone in the Attic

Hurricane Katrina

Last night she was a hurricane
exhaling tornadoes.
When she knocked,
old woman did not answer, and she
threw trees at her front door like arrows.

This morning Katrina is a woman in a black hat,
singing calm bayou spirituals as the old woman sits
in her eye.
Songs that never left this low country.
Hymns make you accept your time to go.
Especially a tired old woman who outlived her
children.

Last night Katrina's breath could not take her.
She climbed higher by candlelight.
This made Katrina angry.
She is fast rising water now,
shouting profanity and the old woman's name.

Third night no rescue for her.
Woman sits alone in the attic—
a hot black space.
She saw her death in a dream on the first night
while hiding in the bathtub.

Rising water cools her.
An old photo of her mother
sails to her hand.
Mother wears a white dress and a red Easter flower,
holds baby girl in her young arms.

As water fills the empty darkness in her attic,
she thinks of nothing but Mother's touch.
Woman sings her childhood lullaby
and rocks gently as floodwater pours in
through the rafters over old woman
and her mother.

Horses of Assateague

Last Wednesday of every July
she waits in beginning morning
nautical twilight to witness
horses swim through a
channel at Chincoteague.

Sun-colored manes bobbing
along Virginia's eastern shore.
They swim through crab pots,
clam shoals, onto low
tide oyster beds,
a graveyard of sunken ships,
history herded by firefighters
of the Chesapeake Bay.

These saltwater cowboys push horses
that were once pirate's loot
aboard a Spanish galleon bound for
black mines in the deep hollers of
West Virginia.

Bodies of Water

He and his brother fish sixty miles off Atlantic coast
for shark, which they do not like to eat.
They are sick from hundred-degree heat
and smell of cut bait, diesel fuel, and saltwater.
Fishing trip is a gift celebrating brother's retirement
from army—Vietnam, El Salvador, Iraq, Kosovo.

His brother awakens to tell him a large tornado
stares at the boat like an angry whale.
He removes seasick face from plastic,
looks up to make eye contact with the demon.
He admires her graceful dance between
clouds and water.

She creates herself and stands erect on ocean's skin.
She drinks sea from a straw and evolves into a
living being. As the monster pulls the boat closer,
he wonders if God really knows his name.
He steps out onto the deck and puts his hand forward,
waiting for her to get close enough to touch or take.

First time he begins to sense what brother
must have felt as a teenager in Southeast Asia—
to live or die on luck, waiting for God to spit
life, death, or waterspouts into innocent, young
bodies of water.

Pier Fishing
Emerald Isle, NC

October pier fills with ordinary people
from driftwood shore to end of last beam.
White wheeled coolers follow.
Few empty slots on gray planks.

New friends line the wood frame
shoulder-to-shoulder, waiting
for high tide and schools
to come together like rising layer cake.

Falling Through Ice

It is a winter night in Southern woods.
He is disoriented like a pilot who has lost the
horizon. Snow fell all day and into evening.
As he walked across a frozen river,
ice opened its skin and pulled him
into darkness by ankles. He fell through,
took his last breath as his face joined
his body underneath ice.

As he sinks, hole above him
fades and appears
to seal itself from the moon.
He remembers watching night snowfall from
windows while standing on his mother's bed.
In the street light, snow is magnified and
hypnotic. Sometimes a gentle breeze lifts
snow in light and causes it to flutter like moths.

He begins to swim in a direction
that could be upward to look
for a hole in blind, black water.

Outer Banks

A barrier from storms,
refuge for the mind,
neither part of the mainland
nor island of its own.

A place we go to pet
the mysterious eyewall of a hurricane
to feel skin of a churning mass
or stare from a curious distance
at the fiery outer ring of a black hole.

A place to see what others see,
feel what others feel, and understand why
we are all "others" ... afraid to get too close,
sucked in, and flung into another world
for the first time, returning differently
or not at all.

People

Woman of Rwanda

Armed men escort European tourists
to see endangered species of mountain gorilla.

They play with offspring in a bamboo
thicket on wooded mountain faces.

A Tutsi woman begins a journey
through valley grass for two buckets
of fresh water near the home of the silverback.

None has survived captivity.
Many believe they die of depression
in the first one hundred days.

Two Hutu soldiers delay her on this simple trip for water.
On her knees, then on her back for them,
each day, for water.

When it starts, she is quiet. She keeps
her eyes open and stares at the mountain
tree tops above the grassy valley.

She thinks about her husband and brothers,
one million in one hundred days of genocide,
their dances, feasts, weddings, and faces.

When it is over, she thinks of the mountain
gorilla and how fortunate they are to live
close to water.

Sandals in the Field
The taking of Nigerian schoolgirls

In the Mandara Mountains of Nigeria
the forest is drained by seasonal streams
that feed the Yedseram and Ngadda Rivers.

In the savannah below, monkey bread trees
with unusually fat, strong trunks appear
randomly in the light of a million constellations.
The eyes of a black panther often
rest on the tree's lower canopy at night.

By day, their canopies provide shade
for the dry backs of the bush elephant
that curiously watched trucks carry
347 kidnapped teenage Chibok schoolgirls
away from a village of mixed religions.

When the parents arrived at the school yard,
they found nothing but hundreds
of girls' sandals in a sparse dry field
among a few red bushwillows.

The children were force-marched through
thorny brush and miles of darkness.
Some girls jumped from the bed of the truck
and the bed of Boko Haram's child soldiers.
Some were killed by the Al-Qaeda trained insurgents
for refusing to convert—religion, social identity, sexual
preferences.

Their dreams to become nurses, mothers,
teachers, doctors, and free were strong.

In exchange for their colorful dresses
and beautiful head scarfs,
the girls now wore a black or gray hijab,
revealing their white teeth
and eyes sunken into dark emotionless faces.

In the Sambisa Forest, the girls sat huddled
together as one chador, listening to the sounds
of the African collard dove singing in the terrorist
refuge.

The girls were waiting to be assigned
a job, husband, and religion.
Boko Haram leader, Abubakar Shekau,
says he was told by Allah to remove the girls from
school, rape, batter, convert, and sell them.

Some of the girls were so ashamed and brainwashed
from their rape, beatings, and abuse that after
escaping, they refused to come home to
the primitive stigma of a girl who had been taken
multiple times every day, some pregnant
and some with children of the caliphate.

Only little men fear the awesome power
of educated women in an emerging world,
here or there.

The Unexplainable Behavior of Birds

Hand-held eyes stand on wooden deck
thirsty for stain.
An old man lifts the eyes into hands and
examines lenses like rare coins.

He untangles strap as a flock of 100 loud
ravens land in front of a young, dark man
standing with the old man's daughter.
She is happy.

He used the binoculars to watch birds on
marshlands around Lake Waccamaw with his
daughter and discussed the rules
migrating birds follow to avoid collisions.

His grandfather used the lenses
long ago to follow field men
cropping his tobacco
in Bertie County.

He focuses but still sees the world in two colors.
His mother told him it should be this way,
another simple rule to avoid collisions
and explain the mystery of birds.

Binoculars lowered to his chest. He thinks
about things once far away from daughter
that now appear closer
without his wooden eyes.

An unfamiliar red bird lands in the field of ravens.
Black birds become silent shadows to the one.
Old man tries to focus with his own eyes
on the unexplainable behavior of a free red bird.

The Perfect Day
Lake Jocassee, SC 1998

Final moments of dusk shroud this mountain
lake and move upon us swiftly like sleep.
We launch and follow fading light
of a distant boat,
looking for her husband and children.

Light disappears.
The sky and water are one black canvas.
We are lost on the lake,
searching wet darkness for familiar campfire.
Each one fades faster than morning dreams.

Hand-held headlight shakes with her nerves
on the deep water in front of us.
Five feet of visibility feels like a waterfall
beneath us. We are confused by the light
and lose the horizon.

Cove after cove search fails.
We yell her husband's name and mountains
throw it back at us as echoes.
We run aground on an accidental beach,
a small island surfaced by low rainfall.

She helps me build the tent like an imaginary wife.
We crawl into small space on water's edge,
surrounded by dark crevasses and driftwood.
Sounds of wind slapping water against rock
lull us into sensible boundaries. We sleep.

Sitting on a boulder, I watch morning rise above night.
Soon someone will find us, or we will find someone.
We are in no hurry for either.
I stand black binoculars on flat rock,
open a book of Mary Oliver and begin to read.

The woman in my tent awakens—smiles,
sits on ground between our site
and beached boat.
She rubs pale feet happily in sand,
fearing nothing but being found too soon.

We are lost in the perfection of this day.
It stares at us like the moment of a comet,
and we are holding onto its tail
long enough to witness the beauty of friendship,
absence of worry, needs, or time.

I realize the intimate peace of knowing
someone this way, even if she is
another man's wife and it is only for a few
brief, innocent moments of life.

Hanging Sheetrock
Manhattan 1978

I'm fifteen, working minimum wage construction.
Today, building a penthouse for a rich high-rise
landlord who walks around each floor
barefoot, bare chest, smoking marijuana. He wears
a thick gold rope chain and cut-off jean shorts.
He greets his employees with a sincere
morning buzz, chocolate bagel breath, and a smile.

He shakes hands with everyone on his second
floor jewelry factory, thanking them for deciding
to come to work this morning, not stealing his gold,
not swallowing his diamonds, or smoking his
marijuana growing on the rooftop.
He comes to me without short-term memory.

Hands me my paycheck
and a cheap beer for being
crazy enough to hang sheetrock
while standing on
the ledge of a sixteen story building.
I take a break on the ledge.
My heels stare down on 28th Street.

I finish my beer, check my check, and listen
to Santana sing "You've Got to Change Your
Evil Ways" on a silver Walkman radio with a
coat hanger antenna.

Colored Beaches

Atlantic Beach, SC 1954

She was the original Black Pearl,
a Colored Only beach carved
out of blue sky for people
who loved the white salt
enough to get their hair wet.

You could dance free,
feel cool, human,
and know where rainbows
end for colored folk.

Atlantic Beach, South Carolina, purchased by prominent African Americans in the 1930s, was one of only a handful of beaches on the east coast where African Americans were allowed. They nicknamed the beach The Black Pearl.

Beneath Charleston

He walks through dark
parking garage beneath
rich downtown Charleston.
He passes three Hispanic ladies
taking a break from cleaning hotel rooms.
For these ladies every day is Tuesday.

A woman and her husband laugh
in each other's arms as they walk
across the eyes of the three invisible women.
The man wears a pressed white cotton shirt,
red tie, Bostonian wingtips making rhythmic
crisp sliding sounds across concrete.

Corporate friends upstairs
laughing, eating well, uncorking
fresh bottles of expensive wine.
It is a Christmas party.

He hears a glass break and
turns to see three sets of swollen ankles
resting on a bench against the wall.
The Latina woman on the right is rubbing the
back of her friend who is stung
by the confusion of an epileptic seizure.

She sits quietly, not blinking,
trapped in the mental exhaustion greeting
her at the end of each paralyzing episode.
She has had them since childhood.

She was tired from scrubbing bathtubs and
making beds that sit too low to the ground.
Tired from picking up heavy wet towels
off bathroom floors and scrubbing dry spit
from sinks while worrying about her children
walking home alone from the bus stop.

Swings

No one swings here in winter.
North wind in your face.
Frozen mud puddles beneath feet.
I want him to push me anyway.

He stands at my back, still wears his work clothes.
Pushes for the first time.
Strong hands against my shoulders
challenging me to go higher.

I point my toes to sky.
Gripping cold steel links,
I drive my legs into the wind,
excited, afraid, protected.

I feel only one hand pushing me.
Now just fingertips.
At my highest point, I reach
for cloud shadows and cloud faces.

Now I feel nothing.
He is not pushing.
I still swing.
Unafraid.
Unprotected.

Villanelle for a Bag Lady
Brooklyn 1979

Before I knew you never wore a bra on rainy days
I wanted to travel can to can, trick or treat year-round with you
before I knew you were a has-been whore and had street ways.

Saw you bathe in a fountain, tear through a large green maze,
change into a new old dress, covering half your body.
I knew you never wore a bra on rainy days!

You spread your legs like little girls in sand, knees raised,
and when muddy and wet, I wanted to play with you
before I knew you were a has-been whore and had street ways.

I wanted to pull your hair, maybe hold your wrinkled hand, play
a cold city night in a garbage can, just us two.
I knew you never wore a bra on rainy days.

Once I saw you steal from a blind boy's vase.
At the Port Authority I saw others like you.
My sister said they were all has-been whores and had street ways.

Even you, to sell your body to Muslims, persuade
a Brownstone Jew, and a gypsy cabbie.
They knew you were a has-been whore and had street ways
before I knew you never wore a bra on rainy days.

All That Shines

A safe barefoot walk down a hot
yellow brick road, first impressions
of new friends, a view from
the tallest building on September 11,
girl next door with eyes like black pearls,
legs like stepladders, mouth like a siren,
petite yellow woman in a catholic church—
sugar in a confession booth, the glitter of
a second wedding dress, the surface
calm of a teal tide sparkling on golden sun
that shines and also rips and burns.

June's Horses

White country home, wooden porch
wrapped around Smithfield.
Horses graze and play
in strong fence and clean pasture.

She sits in a white rocking chair,
her wife leans on a close column.
They talk about diversity of horses
and the roles they play in the herd.

In the pasture, a Mayan-Mexican
woman talks to June's horses.
Spanish speaks to herd's nostrils.
They are happy with the smell
of her language.

A foggy red stable sits quietly
in front of woods, waiting for nightfall's
return of June's horses to rest.
And a more confident immigrant
Mayan mother returns to Mexico.

The Shadow Box Maker

She places small ceramic black dog
on shelf inside her last work.
This is her craft—
an artist of shadow boxes.

She knows he is the one who stops her
from getting dressed. Grabs her in the mirror,
makes her look away. His reflection is at
home in any glass or still water.

He denies her red dresses, white scarves.
His colors—deep purple, distant charcoal.
Stops her from combing hair,
watering flowers, returning mother's phone calls.

He makes her paint with confused color,
distorted warmth, uncontrollable perspective.
He follows her to a daughter's birthday,
husband's office Christmas party.

He does not allow her to dance, sing,
play with children, love with passion.
When she sits on the porch,
he lies quietly at her feet or in shade underneath—
loyal to her—but daring her.

When she tries to smile or tell someone,
he shows his teeth and controls her
like the black dog in the shadow box,
gnawing on her like a bone.

The Black Dog was a term used by President Lincoln to describe his personal bouts with depression.

Sprinter's Parable

Gun sounds.
Head down.
The last sound he will hear until crossing
the finish line—the loneliness of his own
breathing keeping rhythm with spikes
scratching asphalt.

Lift head now.
Remind self to relax at the halfway.
Relax to run faster.

Sound Side of Kitty Hawk

They lie on the sound side of Kitty Hawk.
Water is at peace, flat and wakeless.
She makes handprints in soft sand dunes,
waiting for strong gusts to renew indentations.

She looks over Kill Devil Hills where Wright
brothers gave birth to flight. Gentle lifting breezes
attract sound and color of hang gliders circling
between face and sun.

At this moment, he wants to care about nothing
but sun and men who become kites and land
on rolling, white hills. But he is scared like Dorothy
and thinks click heels and wake up home.

She wants him to put his ear against her stomach
and listen for the sound of water. He rubs his hand
over contours of the tan hill, wonders if any breeze
will be strong enough to lift the prints of this decision.

He watches the last windless glider spiral to earth
like the final leaf of a season and begins to worry
about life after their choice.

Blind Date on Corpus Christi

Her bedroom door is open again.
She lies in bed with a nightlight on.
He unfolds the sofa in the next room
and listens to the ocean.

He wonders if her open door is an invitation
to be rescued from the bad dreams that force
a yellow Black woman with green eyes
to need childhood nightlights.

Without a Witness

In Ketchikan we watch the salmon make the run upstream
before the first snow. At midnight we see and hear
Aurora Borealis.

The sound of color inspires her to tell me who she really is
even though it's been twelve years
since we married in Las Vegas without a witness.

She tells me she was molested by a cousin and two
family friends in Mexico City when she was a child.
Her father was away drinking and playing baseball.
Her mother was trusting, depressed, and alone in
her own suffering.

She tells me she wasn't close to her father because he
drank the money for her Fiesta de Quince Anos,
but it is really because he wasn't there
to stop men from leaving Godless fingerprints
on her childhood.

A Woman Tells Him about Her Rape

She tells him it happened sixteen years
ago at an indoor swimming pool in Rochester.

She feels the grip of many hands
around her wrists. The strength of
larger hands spread legs.
Her long, slender swimmer's limbs
begin to shake.

Voices and faces, too close for focus,
expressionism, distortions. She is disabled.

In the worst of the moment,
she begins to utter a song she
learned in church as a child.
The men back away from her and
fade into the darkness around the door.

Echoing laughter lingers after door slams.
She lies paralyzed on wet ceramic floor.

She feels stabbing throb of persistent competitive sex.
Rolls over into pool, swims slowly through blood water
with open eyes. Pulls painfully toward warm white lights
in pool. Wishes this was the same mysterious
bright light we see at death.

She hugs his pillow, begins to sob.
She was only fifteen when it happened,
and she never told her parents.

Naked Iguana

Spring arrives young in South Carolina.
He sees her reflection through bedroom mirror.
She sits naked on counter in front of sink, singing.

Folds legs and fans knees like butterfly
wings. Her blue eyes inches away from
bathroom mirror.

She listens to radio, admires reflection and
nimbleness. Only woman he has known this
comfortable with her body. She likes herself.

You could ask her age, weight.
He did.
She was proud to tell him.

She is afraid of heights—closes her eyes
and looks away as they exit glass elevator
of a high-rise hotel.

Her mother died when she was twelve.
Father did not want her.
"I lived with an uncle who abused me," she says.

He is a divorced dad with custody. She asks, "Why?"
He could never live without his son.
She smiles. "It is nice to be wanted," she says.

After dinner, he takes her to a nightclub called the
Naked Iguana. Women admire her and want to dance
near her body. They come close behind her.

She makes love when she dances, man or woman.
She squeezes his hand—ready.
They are wet from the dance.

He meets his three-year-old son in North Carolina.
Drives home, alone, to the Shenandoah Valley
through the Blue Ridge Mountains of Virginia.

Still winter in mountains dressed in snow and ice.
They stand shoulder to shoulder.
Everyone admires them.

Her name was Charity.
Nice to be cold and alone again with son,
away from spring that comes too early
in the midlands of South Carolina.

Prizefighter

He looks at once-feared face
in a bathroom mirror before
last fight. Hands taped and
face greased. Eyes sag over
background of butterflies,
blemishes, old cuts.

This is his second comeback,
maybe his third. He's been champion
once, maybe twice. He is from
Philadelphia, New York,
Las Vegas, or Louisville.

His name is Iron something,
maybe it is Sugar somebody.
He's beaten drugs, White hopes,
foreign heroes, and lovers.

He turns from mirror and
bows his head for a humble prayer
in a punch-drunk voice
diminished to half speed.

Prays for arm to rise at sound
of last bell, to be remembered as
champ and forgiven for being
an imaginary hero.

Palm Reader

Second floor of a dark downtown jazz club,
small Japanese woman rolls his fisted fingers
open and prepares to read palm.
They sit together, a table for
two in a loft above crowded bar.

She is no tarot card palm reader, lying to you
about new relationships or money.
She was taught to read palms as a child
by a grandmother in Kyoto who
predicted and survived Hiroshima.

Palm reader tells him to relax hands.
Hard to do when he knows someone
prepares to read his death like weather.
She rubs his palm
while the music plays.

He relaxes.
She tells him she knows jazz,
likes men who know jazz
and aren't afraid of the truth
or consequences of short lifelines.

Paris Heat Wave

summer 2003

Paris introduces him to a woman named Claustrophobia.
This small hotel room was built for less than one.
Maybe it was the last home for a suicidal impressionist
or a heroin addict trumpet player.

If they lived in his room during summers like this,
surely, they would believe today is a good day to die
of an overdose or to cut off an ear.

It's the worst ever heat wave here.
There is no air conditioner. He is exhausted
from a long walk from the Louvre.
He lies down naked and drowns in the sweat of his bed.

White sheets outline his body like canvas. He is in a seascape
somewhere between sleep and consciousness.
His thoughts make no sense.

He stares at the face of Notre Dame and imagines
the sun's fire melting her stone, wood, and art.
Mona Lisa followed him from the museum.
Her eyes bear down on him—she wants something.

Hotel drips, becomes steamy. He examines the last drop
clinging underneath the left shutter of his window. It swells
with juice of a stream flowing from top of frame.

The drop swells more and stretches. Fat nipple of water snaps,
descends two stories to explode on sidewalk. The silent burst
occurs between a man passing a woman as he looks back at
her walking in a tight, white, short skirt and black stilettos.

He lies down on the bed to begin a drift on the Rhine River. The wife of Gioconda closes her eyes, fades into Da Vinci's background.

He begins to cool off by forgetting about hot Notre Dame but not about the sound of a butcher's knife cutting through a cold, fat Carolina watermelon. Red juice drips off his chin as he holds the rind in hands, eats with face as Notre Dame stops smoldering and welcomes the rainfall.

Church Women

Grandmother sits on the front row
saying "Praise God" to everything
our preacher says. He says next Sunday
will be his last sermon as our minister,
and my grandmother says, "Praise God."

When a new young man with broad shoulders
and a deep voice joins the church,
the young women of the church say,
"Praise God."

Pastor asks little girl if she wants to
go to heaven. She says, "No, I want to
go to McDonalds." Her big sister says,
"Praise God."

When the woman sitting behind me ran
down the aisle of our Methodist church
like a Free Will Baptist, shaking her hair and
anything not tied down or strapped in,
the men of the church shouted, "Praise God."

When the tall, dark preacher gets excited and
begins to sweat, the women of the church
get hot and begin to fan.
Hats and tight dresses rock in pews
and the ladies shout, "Praise God, praise God."

Reading to Small Children

They gather in the loft
above the classroom,
mouths open like nesting
baby birds waiting to be fed.

Open the book
and they hold heads up,
open ears and big
brown, blue, and green eyes.

They hang onto your words
with hands and ears.
They trust a man who needs
them more than they need him.

My son sits in the middle
of the children, not knowing
that I may lose him tomorrow.

Between Raindrops

A small girl runs out of mother's
storm door into the yard, barefoot.
Holds face and palms skyward.
Closes eyes.
Opens mouth.
Holds tongue out into rain.
Little, cool drops splash face.

When eyes are open,
she smiles at spaces
between raindrops.
Tastes the sweet and sour of water
like the pitter-patter of miracles and tragedies
that will frame a fully digested life.

Jazz in the Dark

This is music.
Puts me in mood,
not to love, laugh,
nor mood for woman's touch
or another man's voice.
Just mood to live.
There is peace in the mood to live.
No hurt, no end of laughter,
just mood to live
in emotionless peace.

American Jazz on a French Horn

First time he plays in France,
he blows at the club Caveau de la Huchette.
Parisians look at him like bad manners.
American Jazz on a French horn.
This is not jazz—it is Quebecois.

But the French horn is his natural
voice, not the one God gave him.
When he yawns or sneezes,
an impulsive string of sound leaps
from parted lips like cartoon slang
in an animator's bubble.
Beautiful, deep, alluvial.

Maybe surgeons should implant
French horn sounds in the man
who lost his voice box to cancer.
Let him speak sad jazz virtuosos.
Remove that mechanical
Darth Vader-like thing that makes
little girls hide behind the shield
of a mother's skirt when he says,
"Hello, beautiful."

Louis Armstrong

Face swells
trumpet blows
with the force
of the Chinese
autumn tidal bore.

Sleeping with Poets –
Elizabeth Barrett Browning

Elizabeth sits on edge of the bed.
He grabs her words, pulls her next to him.
She understands every man's requirements
and for that reason, every man wishes
that he was her lost saint. He confesses to her
that his debt is to listen to her words with
the collective passions of all his life.

She comes to him willingly and without pseudonym
because he knows her suffering—
the oppression she witnesses
at hands of men, her own sensitivity
for the cry of children and destiny of the poor.
He understands the death of her brother,
the wrath of an angry father,
and the childhood illness that gives her poetry
life and takes it away like a controlling lover.

She knows it will eventually kill her.
Yet, she sleeps with him because she believes
with all her heart that he shares her
conviction to die a poet, even if their
destiny is death by words.

Sleeping with Poets – Emily Dickinson

Emily admires leaves falling from his bedroom window.
She writes of loneliness and love lost in nineteenth
century New England.

Her face is a simple, younger *Whistler's Mother*, iconic.
She is not what others would call beautiful.
She is more than beauty.

She believes that he is not most men.
Most would not know the sensitivity of her shy soul
or the depth of her explosive writing fueled by fear
and the hurt of a lover's abandonment.

His mind and heart are drawn
to her empathy for the impoverished.
They both understand why the rich want to believe
the poor are happy enough.
In return, she accepts his conditions for love.
Emily submits pen to passion
and her needs to him.

Sleeping with Poets – Phillis Wheatley

Tonight, he sleeps with Phillis.
She arrived in this country
from shores of Africa aboard
a slave schooner for which she
is named. She is the only woman
he knows who can summon both Greek
and Latin gods when they lie down
together to experience passion.

She trusts him. Begins to whisper moistly
in his ear. Tells him the story of a hurricane
she witnessed in North Carolina in 1772.
It descended from the heavens like Aeolus
riding down on her in a chariot.

She is a poet who creates her world,
one more socially acceptable than a
Black woman's life in 1773 Boston.

He reminds her that to lie down with him
is not adultery. Her master's son,
Nathaniel Wheatly, is gone now and
can take her no more. He has left her soul
and elegies to him.

He tells her that with him she is always
human, free, and enough.

Catching Ghost Minnows

On a pathless field in old Green Swamp
a mother and son walk barefoot
searching for a sandy creek in the woods.

A field of blue Venus flytraps grow
in the understory among wild cinnamon ferns.
Son and mother use toes to tease the trigger hairs
between the leaves of the toothy plant.
The blind carnivore does not react.
It dies if it misses.

Mother and son walk into the clear creek and press
a silver bucket against a thick root
to ambush a school of ghost minnows
in their watery part of the world.

She lifts the container of racing flesh
from flow and sound of the stream.
The creek darkens from the stir of the bucket.

The boy's swift right hand follows his eyes into vessel.
He tries to catch darting minnows.
His mother tells him to close his eyes,
use a slower left hand to feel
the soft flesh swim between calm fingers.
Now lift a minnow from the steel pail.

It is mindful faith, not skill and sight,
that enables both to prevail.

Evaporation

She meticulously unravels
ball of hurried and
wrinkled Saran.

Middle class kid
stares at slices of
damp carrot wedges.

Thought of eating,
gaining another pound.

Remembers she can
get rid of it.

Hoping nobody notices
means of thin frame.

Looks like a child
who did not make
Schindler's List.

In a few weeks, she will
not have to worry
at all.

Flower Gatherer

She wades through low country
swamp and brackish tide, wears
leather chaps to protect against
moccasins and alligators.

She pulls a wooden red canoe blooming
with flowers. Loads the open floating vase
with rare colorful plants, some timeless
prehistoric cattails to tuck in with puppy's breath
and rare Bells of Ireland back in her shop.

Cat-fishermen and guides on the Santee
Cooper search for monstrous blues
and schools of stripers. They power slow-
moving pontoon boats, gaze at a familiar
woman wading through shallow
waters of a wooded marsh. They respectfully
slow their wake and wave to silver hair.
She returns a smile.

Woman pulls canoe with a hand-made
rope matching her long, thick braid.
She passes old plantation homes lined
with pecan trees and Spanish moss.
Once floodwater for slaved rice fields long ago,
now blooms a nautical bouquet for this brave
woman who makes a living searching for flowers
in colorful fields of alligators.

Sweet Tea

Two salesmen are in Eastern North Carolina near Raleigh,
a town called Zebulon. They ride in white pickup truck
and tell each how excited they are to work together.

The White man carries a small cooler filled with ice and cold
sweet tea. He hands the Black man a Styrofoam cup.
They ride and eat chopped pork barbecue sandwiches with
coleslaw and hot sauce. They drink sweet iced tea.

They continue down the highway.
Tulips and wild flowers line pine woods along the route
like wallpaper covering the truth.

The salesmen meet a man called Jeremiah.
He is not pleased to see the White salesman.
As the two men approach Jeremiah, he asks both
to leave and tells the Black salesman he will never
buy from him again.

The White salesman says Jeremiah got angry with him
because he was in the Ku Klux Klan.

"Why didn't you tell me?" asked the Black salesman.
"I didn't think you would work with me
if I told you I was in the Klan—it was a long time ago."

They quietly ride back to Raleigh, sipping sweet tea.
The White salesman listens to a Southern Baptist minister
on AM radio. He asks the Black man what he thought
about the barbecue, and, with the preacher shouting
through the static, he asks the Black man if he is born again.

The Black salesman stares out of the window of the truck
and wonders what these small towns were like in the sixties,
if the White salesman ever lynched Black folk, and
understanding why the tea in the South has to be very sweet.

Shatterproof

A bronze girl dares the Wall Street Bull.
She wears a metal shield dress.
Hands are on hips.
Elbows locked.
Ponytails tight.
Without the red maleta, she will challenge
every man who tries to gouge her identity
or pierce her body with pointed words
or unwelcomed acts of power and prejudice.
Unflinching, the girl is shatterproof.

About the Author

Horace McCormick Jr. lives in Harnett County, North Carolina. He studied creative writing at East Carolina University and attended graduate school at the University of Dallas. Horace served as an intelligence officer in the army after college. He later worked and taught at the University of North Carolina at Chapel Hill. Horace does most of his writing on Oak Island, North Carolina,  and in Mexico City where he met his wife, Sara.

The Color of Water is his first book of poetry. Horace's writing explores differences among people around the world. Horace combines his interest in understanding "differences" with art and nature—water in particular—to create greater self-awareness and empathy for every culture's battle with human suffering and emotional well-being.

Horace's writing is influenced by having spent most of his time in the woods on a reservoir while growing up near the Fort Bragg military base during the Vietnam War.

Horace's next book, The Devil's Courthouse, is a collection of short stories that explores the intersections of Latin American, African American, and Native American experiences in the United States. The provocative short stories in this book beautifully portray life from the Outer Banks to the Smokey Mountains of North Carolina in the nineteenth and twentieth centuries. The book is scheduled for publication in early 2021. When Horace is not writing, he is usually fly-fishing the sounds around the Outer Banks, wading in a stream for trout somewhere in the Appalachian Mountains, or fishing in his backyard for bluegill with his children Maya and Austin.

Made in the USA
Middletown, DE
30 December 2020